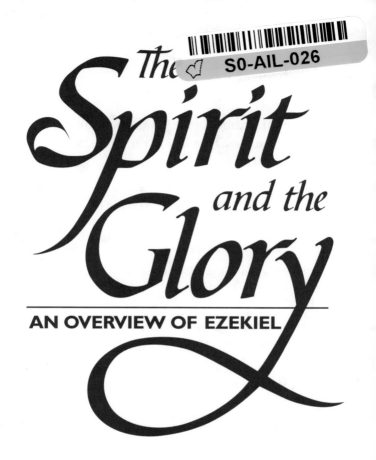

The Spirit and the Glory

AN OVERVIEW OF EZEKIEL

JACK HAYFORD
SCOTT BAUER • JACK HAMILTON

THE SPIRIT AND THE GLORY
A Practical, Introductory Guidebook for a
Comprehensive Overview in the Bible Book
of EZEKIEL

Copyright © 1997 Living Way Ministries.

Unless otherwise noted, all Scripture references are from the
New King James Version:
Copyright © 1979, 1980, 1982 by Thomas Nelson, Inc.,
Nashville, Tennessee.
Maps and illustrations taken from the *Nelson's Complete Book of
Bible Maps and Charts*, ©1993, Thomas Nelson, Inc. Used by
permission.
Outline of Ezekiel taken from the *Spirit-Filled Life Bible*,
©1991, Thomas Nelson, Inc. Used by permission.
Pictorial summary of Ezekiel taken from *What the Bible Is All
About*, ©1986, 1989 by GL Publications. Published by Regal
Books. Used by permission.

Photographs of Dr. Jack Hayford, Dr. Scott Bauer, and
Dr. Jack Hamilton by Christopher Glenn Photography.

Published by Living Way Ministries
14300 Sherman Way
Van Nuys, CA (USA) 91405-2499
(818) 779-8400 • (800) 776-8180

ISBN 0-916847-23-3
Printed in the United States of America.

TABLE OF CONTENTS

Introducing the Bible Book of **Ezekiel**   5

Outline of **Ezekiel**   7

Part 1:
  **The Pillar Principles of
  Ezekiel**   9

Part 2:
  **The Relevant Answers in
  Ezekiel**   29

Part 3:
  **Practical Wisdom From
  Ezekiel**   45

Let's Look at Ezekiel   59

Ministry Resources   66

*If this is your first use of the Bible Book-a-Month study
guide, read pages 64-65.*

EZEKIEL

KEY WORD: "THE FUTURE RESTORATION OF ISRAEL"

The general purpose of Ezekiel was to remind those born during the Babylon exile of the reason for Israel's current destruction, of the coming judgment on the nations of the gentiles, and the coming national restoration of Israel.

KEY CHAPTER: EZEKIEL 37

KEY VERSES: EZEKIEL 36:24–36

"For I will take you from among the nations, gather you out of all countries and bring you into your own land. Then I will sprinkle clean water on you, and you shall be clean… I will give you a new heart and put a new spirit within you… I will put My Spirit within you and cause you to walk in My statutes, and you will keep My judgments and do them. Then you shall dwell in the land that I gave to your fathers; you shall be My people, and I will be your God… I will call for the grain and multiply it… And I will multiply the fruit of your trees and the increase of your fields… Then the nations which are left all around you shall know that I, the Lord, have rebuilt the ruined places and planted what was desolate. I, the Lord, have spoken it, and I will do it."

EZEKIEL

Author:	Ezekiel
Date:	593 B.C. – 573 B.C.
Theme:	Destruction of Jerusalem and Its Restoration
Key Words:	Judgment, Blessing, Individual Moral Responsibility

AUTHOR

The author, whose name means "God Strengthens," is identified as "Ezekiel the priest, the son of Buzi" (1:3). He was probably a member of the Zadokite priestly family that came into prominence during the reforms of Josiah (621 B.C.). He was trained in the priesthood during the reign of Jehoiakim, was deported to Babylon in 597 B.C., and settled in Tel Abib on the Chebar Canal near Nippur (1:1). His ministry briefly overlapped Jeremiah's.

DATE

Ezekiel's call came to him in 593 B.C., the fifth year of Jehoiachin's reign. The latest date given for an oracle (29:17) is probably 571 B.C., making Ezekiel's ministry twenty years long. Exiled in the second siege of Jerusalem, he wrote to those yet in Jerusalem about its imminent and total destruction, including the departure of God's presence.

THE SCOPE OF
EZEKIEL'S PROPHECIES

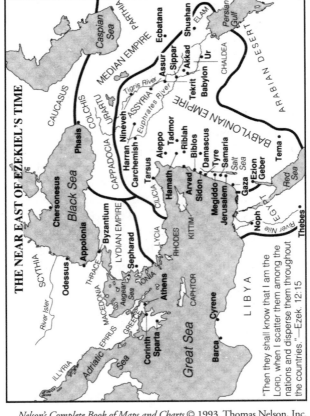

Nelson's Complete Book of Maps and Charts © 1993, Thomas Nelson, Inc.

An Outline of
EZEKIEL

**I. The opening vision and call
    of Ezekiel**   **1:1–3:21**
     A. Introductory visions   1:1–28
     B. The prophet's commission   2:1–3:21

**II. Prophecies and visions of Jerusalem's
     destruction**   **3:22–24:27**
     A. Oracles of judgment   3:22–7:27
         1. Against Jerusalem   3:22–5:17
         2. Against the whole nation   6:1–7:27
     B. Visions of idolatry in the temple   8:1–11:25
     C. Judah's exile and captivity   12:1–24:27
         1. Messages of judgment
             against Judah   12:1–19:14
         2. Oracles before the fall
             of Jerusalem   20:1–24:27

**III. Oracles of doom against foreign
      nations**   **25:1–32:32**
     A. Against Ammon   25:1–7
     B. Against Moab   25:8–11
     C. Against Edom   25:12–14
     D. Against Philistia   25:15–17
     E. Against Tyre   26:1–28:19
     F. Against Sidon   28:20–26

    G. Against Egypt   29:1–32:32

IV. Prophecies of restoration   33:1–48:35
    A. Ezekiel as watchman   33:1–33
    B. God as shepherd   34:1–31
    C. Judgment against Edom   35:1–15
    D. Restoration of Israel   36:1–37:28
    E. Judgment against Gog   38:1–39:29
    F.   Restoration of the Temple   40:1–46:24
    G. Restoration of the Land   47:1–48:35

PART 1

THE PILLAR PRINCIPLES OF EZEKIEL

JACK HAYFORD

EZEKIEL'S TEMPLE

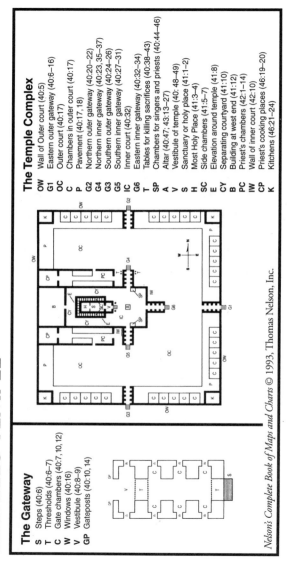

The Gateway

- **S** — Steps (40:6)
- **T** — Thresholds (40:6–7)
- **C** — Gate chambers (40:7, 10, 12)
- **W** — Windows (40:16)
- **V** — Vestibule (40:8–9)
- **GP** — Gateposts (40:10, 14)

The Temple Complex

- **OW** — Wall of Outer court (40:5)
- **G1** — Eastern outer gateway (40:6–16)
- **OC** — Outer court (40:17)
- **C** — Chambers in outer court (40:17)
- **P** — Pavement (40:17, 18)
- **G2** — Northern outer gateway (40:20–22)
- **G4** — Northern inner gateway (40:23, 35–37)
- **G3** — Southern outer gateway (40:24–26)
- **G5** — Southern inner gateway (40:27–31)
- **IC** — Inner court (40:32)
- **G6** — Eastern inner gateway (40:32–34)
- **T** — Tables for killing sacrifices (40:38–43)
- **SP** — Chambers for singers and priests (40:44–46)
- **A** — Altar (40:47; 43:13–27)
- **V** — Vestibule of temple (40: 48–49)
- **S** — Sanctuary or holy place (41:1–2)
- **H** — Most Holy Place (41:3–4)
- **SC** — Side chambers (41:5–7)
- **E** — Elevation around temple (41:8)
- **CY** — Separating courtyard (41:10)
- **B** — Building at west end (41:12)
- **PC** — Priest's chambers (42:1–14)
- **IW** — Wall of inner court (42:10)
- **CP** — Priest's cooking places (46:19–20)
- **K** — Kitchens (46:21–24)

Nelson's Complete Book of Maps and Charts © 1993, Thomas Nelson, Inc.

THE PILLAR PRINCIPLES OF
EZEKIEL

The prophecy of Ezekiel literally *spins* into our view when we open its pages! We are instantly thrust into partnership with the prophet as he describes his call; a bewildering vision of the glory of God—a description which has over and over conjured notions of *flying saucers* to the minds of readers.

Thereby, we are dramatically introduced to a prophet whose passion unfolds before our eyes, proceeding from this stirring wake-up call to ministry to include a spread of emotions evoked by events and visions that include:

- <u>The pain of watching the fall</u> of his nation and its capital, Judea and Jerusalem, and hearing of their devastation from a distant land where he has been taken captive.
- <u>The agony of experiencing the death</u> of his wife, and being directed by God to disallow himself the release of any public display of grief, in order to speak to his hearers by this prophetic picture.
- <u>The hope of seeing a vision</u> of Israel's restoration from destruction and death as a nation— the famous *Valley of Dry Bones* imagery—which describes spiritual renewal as well as national recovery.

- The comfort of being given the expectation of an ultimate Temple in Jerusalem, where the glory of God, which had abandoned his people because of sin, will come again to abide —*God is Present!*

There is an agony and an ecstasy to Ezekiel—a case of human failure plummeting to the depths of pain and loss, joined to the promise of a divine grace restoring a people to the heights of purpose and destiny. Both the devastating fall and the ultimate restoration of Israel are born of the same holy power—*the Spirit and the Glory*; the Person of the Holy Spirit of God, manifesting the holy purpose and presence of God. Ezekiel makes clear that God's Glory will not abide where sin and rebellion persist, but he makes equally clear that God's Spirit is tirelessly at work to re-breathe life into people and settings where sin's death-syndrome has previously dominated.

This Time in History

It is six centuries before the birth of Jesus, and a welter of activity swirls on the international scene at the time of Ezekiel's rise to ministry. It is helpful to capture a sense of this setting; a maze of events involving the super-powers of Babylon, Assyria, and Egypt. Like other smaller nations of the time, the Jews were tossed on the rising and falling tides of the intense struggles between these three, and it is upon this stage that Ezekiel's prophecy is set.

The prophet was among the exiles taken from Jerusalem in 597 B.C., and we find him "among the captives by the River Chebar." To maximize the resources of the Euphrates River, a canal system was developed around the ancient city of Babylon, and Chebar was a part of this—a waterway which was southeast of the city in the region of Chaldea. Politically speaking, Ezekiel's situation was the result of the upheaval among empires that had taken place, amid which his own people had become lost as pawns on the chess board of world events.

Only eight years before, Nebuchadnezzar, the feared warrior-king of Babylon, had crushed Egypt's forces at the battle of Carchemish (606 B.C.). It was there the Babylonians established their dominance over Egyptian powers in the region and achieved the final demise of Assyria.

Assyria had known world dominance for centuries, during which time they had vanquished the northern kingdom of Israel (the ten tribes) in 723 B.C. But now, the southern kingdom (Judah—the two tribes) had been subjugated, for shortly before Carchemish, Nebuchadnezzar had established his claims in the region as he laid siege to and conquered several cities, including Jerusalem (606 B.C.). It was there, in Judah's captial that he installed a puppet king from the Jewish kingly line—Jehoiakim (who is not to be confused with Jehoiakin, his son who later became king for three months). At the same time, he took thousands of Jews as hostages to Babylon. This group included Daniel the prophet, who was then a young man (Daniel 1), but who in intervening years established a reputation for godliness that Ezekiel notes (Ezekiel 14:14, 20).

At this time, while not as powerful as Babylon,

Egypt was still a force to be reckoned with. So it thus appears that Israel's geographic setting—between Babylon's realm of control to the north and east, and Egypt's kingdom to the southwest—was what likely suggested the possibility of a successful rebellion by the Jews, who chafed under Nebuchadnezzar's yoke.

In 598 B.C., the now-not-so-puppet-like Jehoiakim rebelled against Nebuchadnezzar, hoping to find freedom by playing their southern enemy (Egypt) against their northern oppressor (Babylon). The tactic failed (Jeremiah had predicted this— Jeremiah 25:15–32) and within the year, the Babylonian monarch returned to Jerusalem and re-established his control of the city and all Judah (2 Kings 24:1–7). Egypt was permanently pushed back to her boundaries beyond the Sinai peninsula; Nebuchadnezzar took more Jewish hostages (Ezekiel among these) and shortly placed Zedekiah on the throne of Judah (2 Chronicles 36). The eventual *complete* end of Judah and sack of Jerusalem would still be eleven years away. However that end was very much in sight, because unrighteousness was increasing and darkness was deepening in the once-holy-city (2 Kings 25).

All of this unfolds a picture of the environment of Ezekiel's life and ministry. According to chapter 1:1–3, we learn that the prophet's call came "in the fifth year" of Jehoiachin's captivity, which we know to be 593 B.C., since he is the king whom Nebuchadnezzar replaced with Zedekiah. Three things become apparent in light of this fact and the rest of the entire book:
1. Ezekiel was about 25 years old when he and his family were taken captive to Babylon.

2. A Levitical priest began his service (Numbers 4) at age thirty. Since Ezekiel was of the priestly line, his call to the office of a prophet came at the same time he would have been deemed ready for ministry.

3. On the basis of the many chronological references he makes, Ezekiel gives us the precise timing when prophetic "words" came to him. We find Ezekiel's recorded prophecies were given over a 22-year period, from 593 to 571 B.C.

The Scope of These Prophecies

The Book of Ezekiel is divided into three basic parts: his opening prophecies against Judah and Jerusalem (chapters 1–24); his prophecies against the surrounding nations—especially Egypt (chapters 25–33:20); and his prophecies concerning Israel's future (chapters 33:21–48:35). The map on page six indicates the breadth of the geographic spread of Ezekiel's prophetic words.

The prophecies of judgment given in Ezekiel are easier to grasp when an overview of the key dates is available. Please use the following as a chronological grid for your reading.

BC	Event
597	Jehoiachin taken captive from Jerusalem to Babylon.
589-88	The last siege of Jerusalem begins by Babylonians.
588-87	Sometime in this year, Egypt attempts to aid Judah as a spite against Babylon (that was apparently in line with an agreement

between Judah and Egypt). Ezekiel speaks against this (29:1–16).

587   (April) Ezekiel describes defeat of Egypt (31:1–18).

586   (Sept.) The fall of Jerusalem; Babylonians capture Zedekiah.
         (Dec.) Chapter 33:21 tells of this report reaching exiles in Babylon.

585   (March/April) Ezekiel gives lamentation for Pharaoh's/Egypt's fall, and in the light of Jerusalem's fall, calls the Jews to turn unto the Lord (32:1–33:20).

TWELVE KEY CONCEPTS IN EZEKIEL

Though Ezekiel's prophecies are so directly rooted in a time, place, and circumstance, there are timeless principles that abound in this book. First, there are broad principles and insights that help us understand *prophetic ministry*. Second, there are grand and glorious concepts which rise up to instruct us in the *Person and nature of God*. Third, Ezekiel is a profound proponent of *human responsibility and accountability* before God. Fourth, he is a proclaimer of hope concerning *Israel's future*.

REGARDING PROPHETIC MINISTRY

1. The Accountability of the Prophet
In chapters 3 and 33, the Lord describes the

mission He has given Ezekiel as the same as a "watchman." In the ancient world, the security of the city rested on the watchman's shoulders. He was the one to speak warning or peace to the city. By means of this figure, two things become apparent:

(a) The role of a prophet is one of great responsibility. If neglected, it comes at the expense of the prophet's requirement to ultimately stand before God in answer for the souls/lives of those he or she failed to address. Ezekiel's reluctance to speak (2:14–15), even after so dramatic a visitation (chapter 1) and "input" (chapter 2), is the apparent reason for God's emphasis on this issue.

(b) The urgency of God's heart *that the people hear and turn* is clearly present in this insistence. In placing so heavy an accountability upon the prophet to deliver His Word, God is saying, "You only are my avenue of communication, and I don't want any to be lost due to a failure in My Word going forth." <u>It is also instructive that God did not leave the exiles without their own prophetic representative</u>. Let us note His heart for the citizens of Jerusalem, whether at home (hearing Jeremiah) or in Babylon (hearing Ezekiel).

2. The Variety of Styles in Prophetic Delivery

The variety of means used in relating the word of the Lord is an interesting feature of Ezekiel's message. The New Testament shows the *office of a prophet* (Ephesians 4:11) and *the gift of prophecy* (1 Corinthians 14:5, 31) are very, very different (with comparatively few "prophets," but virtually all believers able to prophesy—see Acts 2:17–18). Still, as present-day believers, we can be assisted to respond to "promptings to prophesy" by noting characteristics of prophetic delivery which Ezekiel reveals. Prophetic words:

- come at clear and distinct moments of Holy Spirit-assisted insight—even at times when we are alone—and may be held in the heart until a God-ordained time of delivery (e.g. 8:1; 20:1; 24:1; 26:1; 29:1, 17; 30:20; 31:1, etc.).
- are often given to the individual by means of pictures or visions that unfold an insight or illustrate a point (e.g. 10:1; 11:1; see also Jeremiah 24:1-10).
- are sometimes instigated by an internal hearing of a voice which, by the holiness and sanity of the content, evidences the Holy Spirit is prompting the prophecy by this means (2:1, 2; et al).
- are sometimes to be delivered by dramatizing the essence of the message in some physical way (4:1-17; 5:1-4; see also Isaiah 20:1-6;).
- may sometimes be delivered through analogy, showing the relatedness of a truth as illustrated in a familiar feature of the hearers' daily lives (15:1–4—vine; 16:15–43—harlot; 17:1–10—eagle; 19:1–9—lioness).
- may derive from common or colloquial expressions of the surrounding culture (12:22; 18:2); the "word" being either a challenge or contrast to conventional wisdom, or even possibly an illustration of a valid point (e.g. Acts 17:18; Titus 1:12–13).

- may be born from the throes of the spokesperson's own struggle or illustrated by personal or physical circumstances they experience or endure (24:15-27; see also, Isaiah 7:10–17/8:1–4).

3. The Objective of God's Sovereign Forecasts

One of the most important things to learn about prophecy is that it is not given to become a resource for attempting to predict *timing*. God does not give His word concerning the *certainty of things to come* so that human beings may spend their time attempting to decide *"when!"* This is probably one of the most important things we can learn about the principles of prophecy: Prophetic revelation is to call to action and obedience, to faith and trust in God. It is not to be a source for interesting speculation, curiosity, or passive, intellectualized consideration. (Note Jesus' confirmation of this principle—John 13:19; 14:29.)

Over 70 times in Ezekiel, the Lord says, concerning His Word, that when it is fulfilled, *"then they shall know that I am the Lord!"* The purpose of prophecy is to give advance notice of divinely intended action, so that after it is fulfilled all viewers will see that the Sovereign God is the Omniscient, Almighty God, and that none can resist His will.

REGARDING GOD'S PERSON AND NATURE

4. The Manifestation of His Glory

"This was the appearance of the likeness of the glory of the Lord" (Ezekiel 1:28). With those words,

the prophet summarizes his description of what seems to be the most unusual vision in the Bible, possibly matched by some of John's depiction in Revelation. Ezekiel seems to wrestle with words in an effort to describe a combination of three features:

- The four *living creatures* (obviously the same John sees—Revelation 4) with their multiple faces and mixed animal and human traits. These are cherubim, and are always associated with God's Throne.

- The *movement* of the creatures, who are governed in their direction by "wherever the spirit wanted to go" (v. 20). It is the "appearance of the wheels" (v.14) and the speed with which they move that has raised the question as to whether contemporary UFO sightings are supernatural rather than extraterrestrial. Of course, no one can authoritatively answer this, but the biblical evidence for the appearance of these high level angelic beings is similar in description to what is often said or depicted of UFOs.

- The *radiant brilliance* associated with God's Presence and Throne. Besides the description of flashes of lightning (v. 13), there is a magnificence of rainbow-like beauty (v. 28; see also, Revelation 4:3), as well as an appearance of jewel-like, fiery sparkling (v. 26–27).

The sum of this suggests the <u>awesomeness</u> of a Being <u>wholly transcendent</u> of earth's order or human grasp, yet evidencing traits familiar to our realm. The <u>perfect union</u> of the material-spiritual realm (the visible [wheels] moved by the invisible [spirit]) reveals a Being Who embraces all realms in <u>perfect harmony</u>.

The radiance—especially in beauty—reveals a presence of <u>dynamic energy</u> joined to <u>aesthetic splendor</u>. While the *vision* doesn't reveal the mood or the manner of the One whose "glory" is expressed here, the *message* of the prophecy does: Here is a Being in Whom exacting expectations for righteousness are matched by a fullness of loving concern for His fallible creatures.

5. The Justice and Mercy of His Throne

"I will bring a sword against you..." (6:3) expresses the categorical commitment of God to wreak judgment upon Judah, "because you have multiplied disobedience more than the nations around you" (5:7). The charge is justified not only on the grounds of violations, but on the strength of the fact that due instruction and warning had been provided in God's Word ("My statutes...My judgments"), and that their corrupt ways gave rise to inhuman and destructive practices (16:21; 20:31). The words, "(you) make your sons pass through the fire," verify that the justice of God is prompted by His mercy, not a vendetta or temper tantrum of a mythological Olympian deity.

The sum of the heartbeat of God amid the judgment of Jerusalem characterizes His endless love and everlasting mercy. Read Ezekiel 18:30–32 and note the qualities of mercy which motivate the lament, "Why will you die, O house of Israel!?"

6. The Certainty of His Word's Fulfillment

Ezekiel 12:17–28 takes up the theme of God's answer to the human argument that there is always more time to indulge the flesh, because the wages of sin can always be re-negotiated or postponed.

The prophet, at God's direction, confronts <u>the lie</u>: *"We've still got lots of time, and what God said isn't going to come true anyway!"* (paraphrase, 12:22c). <u>God's answer</u>: No more postponement! The ax is coming down—the fire is going to fall—*now!"*

This guarantee of *quick and certain judgment* is not the only sense in which this text may be applied. It also holds the promise of hope for all who have cried for deliverance, waited through long nights of travail, and wondered if the Father's answer will ever come. The answer is the same: "None of My words will be postponed any more!" (12:28). These are words worthy of a confident *"Hallelujah!"*

REGARDING HUMAN RESPONSIBILITY

7. The Unavoidability of Accountability

Ezekiel 18 is as relevant to our generation as it was to those in ancient Jerusalem. Here was a culture bent on laying the blame for individual failure on the generation before. The proverb in verse 2 essentially said, "What my folks did is why I do what I do. Everything is their fault: I'm not responsible."

Just as then, our "victim-oriented" society jousts with the windmills of the past—blaming heredity, childhood abuses, social or economic disadvantages, and other "received mistreatment" as the source of our personal problems. "Since the source lies else-where," the argument goes, "there is no personal cul-pability on my part: I'm the product, not the problem!" The result of such "jousting" is always the same as with Quixote: you lose! Tilting with the phantoms of the past never solves the problems of the present.

The place of every individual, accountable before God for each one's own actions and failures, is forever settled: Each shall bear his own guilt—and the soul that sins shall die. (Read the entire chapter, and create a list to show the balance in God's readiness to reward as well as to judge.)

8. The Inescapability of Hypocrisy's Harvest

Ezekiel 14 relates God's response to the hypocrisy of the elders of Israel (see chapter 8). Their feigned worship of God, while surrendering themselves to the vilest of demon worship, is about to garner the most frightening harvest imaginable!

God says to Ezekiel: "When they come to ask you for a word from Me, I'll give them an answer! But it won't be Mine!!—I will 'answer them according to the multitude of his idols.'" This horrifying possibility means that God declares He will allow a person to be given deceiving and destructive answers to their questions—the same lie the demons would give... *and He will allow them to think it is His answer!*

In short, it is God's retribution: Live unto the world-spirit, you'll die by the world-spirit! Don't come to Me for quick answers to your problems when you've committed to long-term submission to the Adversary. (See 2 Thessalonians 2:11 regarding this same action of the Almighty during the last days—our days.) There is only one defense against such delusion: Read Jesus' words—John 8:31–32.

9. The Biblical Revelation of a "Dual Reality"

In Ezekiel's pronouncements of judgment on the kingdom of Tyre (chapters 26–28), the largest of the ancient commercial trading giants is confronted—the "Mammon" of that day. It is in chapters 27 and 28 that the prophet addresses the dual reality of (a) a visible, earthly ruler and his evil kingdom, and (b) an invisible, evil angelic ruler who manipulates the affairs of the visible kingdom. Ezekiel 28:11–19 is deemed by many scholars to be a specific description of the fall of Lucifer—Satan (compare with Isaiah 14:12–17).

This is consistent with the "dual reality" revealed in Daniel's discovery (Daniel 9–10), showing there <u>are</u> demon-beings operating behind earthly kingdoms. Observe:

- Jesus' confrontation by the Adversary in the wilderness, as Satan <u>offers control</u> of earthly kingdoms held under his sway (Matthew 4:8–9); and
- Paul's words
    - (a) showing the <u>invisible demonic presence</u> that is actually behind the physical emblem of idols (1 Corinthians 10:20–21) and
    - (b) reminding us our warfare unto the possessing of peoples for the Kingdom of God is not political, but spiritual—<u>wrestling against evil, invisible</u> beings who so often successfully manipulate and control the affairs of men (Ephesians 6:10–19).

Perceiving and responding to this dual reality with spiritual wisdom and practical balance—without superstition or fanatical excess—is essential to spiritual maturity and effectiveness for Christ.

REGARDING ISRAEL'S FUTURE

10. The Promise of Israel's Spiritual Rebirth

What the Lord appeals for in Ezekiel 18:31, "Get yourselves a new heart and a new spirit,"—(God saying, "Get a Life!!")—He prophesies and promises in chapter 36:25–27:

> *"I will give you a new heart and put a new spirit within you; I will take the heart of stone out of your flesh and give you a heart of flesh. I will put My Spirit within you..."*

Through the Gospel, it has become a promise to all who turn to the Living God through Jesus Christ. But before the Gospel of the Kingdom was fully revealed, God made this covenant with His people Israel. Though in His grace He regathers the scattered host of Israel (see 36:24), verse 28 shows that God's prerequisite to their fully possessing their land in peace and prosperity is this: *spiritual renewal.*

11. The Travail of Israel's National Recovery

Ezekiel breathes with the promise of a literal recovery of Israel as a national entity. Chapter 37 reveals this in the classic vision of the dry bones, reassembled and standing—following death and decay. In verse 15–28, the prophecy is so precise that there is no way it can be misconstrued to suggest a fulfillment before our time. *Both* Israel and Judah shall be reunited and recovered. The return from the Babylonian exile only involved Judah, so the "return" of that era does not answer to this or other key prophecies about the Jewish peoples and the last days.

Involved in this last days struggle for recovery will be considerable international ill will and warfare, as shown in Ezekiel 38 and 39. The northern nations identified here clearly answer to regions of the former Soviet Union—in which many states are presently controlled by Muslim majorities. Are we being shown a forecast of the next "showdown" in the Middle East? One never knows, but this is certain: Israel *shall* possess her place in the sun in a land of her own; Israel *shall* experience considerable travail in realizing this; and Israel *shall* come unto spiritual renewal and be a praise to the Living God.

12. The Hope for Israel's Glorious Restoration

How wonderfully this prophecy focusing on "the Spirit and the Glory" concludes, with a renewed people restored to their land and with a new Temple filled with the *"Shekinah"* presence of God! Chapters 40–48 unveil a vision of the ultimate restoration of worship in the Temple at Jerusalem and the ultimate establishment of a political order structured after the will of God. Many see Ezekiel's vision as symbolic, but certain features of his forecast are inescapably real and to be literally expected.

The diagrams on page 10 show that God was specific—both in architectural and geological surveying terms. This cannot be spiritualized. We are dealing with a future we may not be able to imagine, but the reality of the promise is not ours to tamper with or to reduce through theologizing.

Concluding…

Ezekiel is as comforting a prophecy as it is confrontive, and as restorative in its forecast as it is retributive. The balance of God's justice and mercy is seen, and the hope of full renewal and recovery for each soul is within the prophet's vision of possibilities. God's Spirit longs to bring God's glory in fullness to us all, until the temple of our own being is fully indwelt, and it is said of us what will finally be said of Jerusalem—

Jehovah Shammah... The Lord is there!

WHEN
EZEKIEL PROPHESIED

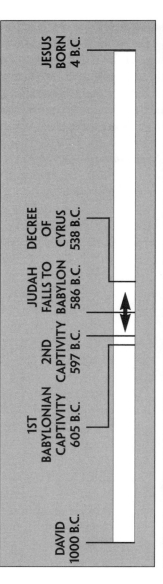

| DAVID 1000 B.C. | 1ST BABYLONIAN CAPTIVITY 605 B.C. | 2ND CAPTIVITY 597 B.C. | JUDAH FALLS TO BABYLON 586 B.C. | DECREE OF CYRUS 538 B.C. | JESUS BORN 4 B.C. |

Ezekiel:

Individuals who neglect their responsibility for their souls must pay a price.

PART 2

THE RELEVANT ANSWERS IN EZEKIEL

SCOTT BAUER

THE HOLY SPIRIT AND
THE NEW COVENANT

Without question, Ezekiel is a book with outlandish imagery, confusing prophetic encounters, and powerful challenges to the people of God. From the dramatic pictures in the opening chapter of the four-faced "living creatures," to wheels-within-wheels filled with eyes, it is a great difficulty to understand the meaning of the prophet and to find where his message fits in the flow of God's purpose for His people. However, the prophet's message does come through with clarity and genuine life-changing power.

The opening segment of the book deals with Israel's judgment and the consequences of its sin. As God is proclaiming the terms of its punishment, there is something else dramatic at work here: the revelation of how the Holy Spirit works in the lives of people and nations. The implications of Israel's national rejection of God and its embrace of idolatry literally push the Holy Spirit from His dwelling place in the Temple. It is the cumulative sin of the nation and its leaders which so pollutes the environment around the dwelling place of the Spirit that there can be no reconciling of the people's sin. The Spirit of God evacuates the Temple (10:18) in possibly the most graphic picture of God's broken heart for His people in all of the Bible.

Yet, the book of Ezekiel offers a second picture of the Holy Spirit's working in the lives of individuals—there is an intimate view of God at work in the life of the prophet, and there is also the promise of His cleansing and abiding presence in any who open to Him. It is a book filled with hope as it defies the stereotyping of the Old Testament by those who would declare it the covenant of law and separated from the work of God's grace. If we will break down our preconceptions of an angry God toward His people, we will see in Ezekiel the consistent unifying force of His grace. We encounter in this book the **"everlasting covenant"** (16:60; 37:26) and **"an atonement for all you have done"** (16:63). These verses redefine the way God works among His people and offer the promise of a "new spirit" as the result of a sensitive response to the Lord (36:26).

The Holy Spirit at Work in a Nation

Since the days of Israel's deliverance from Egyptian bondage, the defining difference between them and their neighbors has been the entertaining of God's Holy Spirit in the life of the nation—from the presence of God in the glory cloud at the Red Sea (Exodus 13:21-22), to the filling of the Tabernacle with His glorious presence (Exodus 40:34), to the permanent place of His residing in the Temple at Jerusalem (2 Chronicles 7:1). The solitary thing that has separated Israel from other nations has been the sovereign presence of God. It has been Israel's responsibility to serve the Lord and to offer itself as the only viable witness of God's mercy and power to the entire world. In the presence of God is the testimony of Israel's unique place in history and the call to serve Him with all their heart.

The Departing Glory (10:18)

At the dedication prayer for the Temple (2 Chronicles 7:1), God immediately filled it with His glory. Without hesitation, with fire and a glory cloud, God's awesome presence filled the Temple. David, Solomon's father, had desired to build the Temple as a permanent place for God to dwell among His chosen people. But, with the Lord's prohibition of David, the task remained for Solomon. God's instantaneous response to the invitation of Israel's king to attend to His "resting place" (2 Chronicles 6:41) demonstrated His complete commitment to His people and His willingness to be present among them. This is sadly contrasted in Ezekiel 10:4. Here, the Spirit of God is leaving the Temple. The drama of the moment is poignantly recorded by the prophet:

"Then the glory of the Lord went up from the cherub, and paused over the threshold of the temple."

It is as if the Lord stopped to look over the place of His residence of 350 years to reflect on the horrors of having to abandon the people who no longer had any desire to love or serve Him. The destruction that followed in the nation not only served the cause of God's righteous judgment, but exacted a price of the Lord Himself who had no desire to destroy His people. "I have no pleasure in the death of the wicked, but that the wicked turn from his way and live. "Turn, turn from your evil ways! For why should you die, O house of Israel?" (33:11)

The Spirit of God is always seeking the way of repentance; in this case, it's the turning of a nation from its sin. The reasons for the judgment are clear. Not only is Israel involved in idolatry (their struggle with idols goes back to Mount Sinai and the giving of the Law in Exodus), but its leaders have advanced their rebellion against God to the next level. They are now committing acts of idolatry in the Temple of God itself!

"There, at the door of the temple of the Lord, between the porch and the altar, were about twenty-five men with their backs toward the temple of the Lord and their faces toward the east, and they were worshipping the sun toward the east." (8:16)

This is the final desecration which insists on God's departure from the Temple. Not only does God now act in fury, but He also acts without pity (8:18).

"Is it a trivial thing to the house of Judah to commit the abominations which they commit here?" (8:17)

The location of the abomination and those committing it, who are the authorized representatives of all the people, have advanced unrighteousness *beyond* the point of mere sinning now, but have taken it to the depths of "grieving the Holy Spirit" (Ephesians 4:30). They are beyond "wearying God" (Isaiah 7:13) and have come to the place described in Genesis 6:3 where God is no longer willing to "strive" with man. In this passage, many believe the issue of striving relates to the abiding presence of God with His people. Here, in Ezekiel 10, God abandons the Temple—never to return to temples made with human hands, but instead to come to us as Emanuel, the Temple of God in human flesh (John 2:19–21), where the sacrifice for sin would be made once and for all.

The Holy Spirit's Call to Intercede

Ezekiel 22:30 issues a call for someone to "stand in the gap" in the midst of the moral compromise of Israel and its impending judgment. The consequence of not responding is clearly stated in verse 31: "Therefore I have poured out My indignation on them." The desire of God was that Israel not be destroyed. When the glory of God departed from the Temple, there was never the divine intent to destroy —but to search for a partner to welcome the Holy Spirit's action in the land through intercessory prayer.

Ezekiel 14 declares a chilling judgment on a nation which "sins against Me by **persistent unfaithfulness**" (verse 13). In fact, the Lord's ferocious anger in Chapter 14 is dramatically shown in relationship to three characters in Israel's history. God's commitment of judgment is so great that "these three men"—Noah, Daniel, and Job—are mentioned four times. In all cases, it is affirmed that if these righteous men had lived in Ezekiel's time, they would have been saved—but their families would not have been delivered. There is no way that the righteousness of even these giants in Israel's history could stay the course of God's great judgment against their own family members.

In the course of God's dealings with Ezekiel on the judgment of the nation, "elders" came to see him (14:1). It is clear that the Lord is doubtful of their motive and is unwilling to be only one of the "gods" they have sought. They are neither repentant of their sin nor concerned about God's dealings with them or the nation. They are simply inquiring of yet another "god." As a result, the Lord declares a peculiar judgment—"I the Lord will answer him who comes, according to the multitude of his idols" (verse 4). In the pursuit of idols, God will not be mocked.

God is unwilling to be one of many competing voices for the attention of a man or a nation. When a people truly seek the one true God, then they are no longer desiring the options of their idols. However, where idolatry persists, the Spirit of God answers the inquirer by "the multitude of his idols."

The resulting confusion is obvious in our world today. The relentless pursuit of foreign gods has brought a "new revelation of tolerance" to the "broad-minded" polytheists who reject one truth, one God, and one way to heaven. Because the people of God have pursued Jesus Christ who is "the way, the truth and the life" with passion, they are viewed by the world as "narrow and intolerant." The Church suffers from the lying lips of the adversaries of God who declare that they have received a bold "new revelation" of universal acceptance and appreciation for all religions—**except for the one that honors the true and living God!**

These are deceived by their own rejection of truth and their pursuit of corrupting idols. They receive the revelation of confusion. God will not compete for our attention—**but He will call for repentance!**

Ezekiel offers a clear pathway for the release of blessing and the healing of a nation—**"REPENT"**! (14:6; 18:30) It sounds like preachers who have traveled the sawdust trail of tent revivals. But there is no other way to escape judgment.

The call to repentance has come to every generation. In our day there is considerable insensitivity in the Body of Christ to the desperate cry of God's Spirit to "stand in the gap" and to call for repentance from national leaders. Much of the Church is slow to intercede in taking its place to turn back judgment.

The fate of Israel reads like a horror story in the book of Ezekiel—but there is hope! God promises a new covenant to all who open to Him. It is a way of eternal life and restoration for any people who will repent and respond to Him.

In fact there is a beautiful passage about God's desire to bring relief to the person who "turns from his sin" (33:14). The message of national judgment in this book is directly linked to individual decisions made by those who are confronted by the demands of a Holy God. It is the righteous disposition of our lives before Him, on His terms, that changes the course of God's appointed judgment on a people and a nation.

The Holy Spirit at Work in an Individual

Both Jeremiah and Ezekiel offer prophecies of hope that link the coming of Messiah and the new covenant of His blessing. There is a new day coming that promises the Holy Spirit's presence at work in the life of the believer. It is a radical departure from the organized pursuits of a religious establishment attempting to administrate God's grace to a society based on a system of sacrifice.

In this complete departure from the traditions of the society, Ezekiel is drawing the people back to a personal, devotional relationship with the God of Israel. The prophet by-passes the national interest in religious pursuit as a matter of culture, tradition, or simple corporate identity for the nation. He focuses on each individual's heart-response before God and invites those who will to respond to His grace.

By the time of Ezekiel, the general state of affection for God in the nation of Israel has suffered greatly. God cannot find an intercessor (22:30), and the national leaders of Israel are defiantly pursuing idolatry. The Lord has been reduced to a mere spot in the pantheon of the gods that all of Israel's neighbors serve. Therefore, the call to personal renewal and response to the living God is particularly significant. The key to revitalizing Israel is not just another national call to repentance, but it requires a personal response to relationship with God.

In the reductionism that comes with formalized national religious pursuits, the pattern of Israel's Temple worship was still retained in Ezekiel's time. The last vestiges to leave the culture were the forms of worship (even if maintained only as a matter of tradition) when they had long since lost any meaning to the nation and its people. Of course, in every generation there was a remnant—those who would have heard the message of Ezekiel and would have responded. Despite this, there was still left the general demise of a spiritual response and personal devotion to God in the nation, and this was what was at the core of Israel's eventual collapse.

This call to personal commitment is not a new concept in the Old Testament. Deuteronomy 10:12 insists that the essence of personal response to God has nothing to do with the systems of sacrifice. It is a matter of loving God with all our heart and soul, and walking in His ways. In Ezekiel's prophecy concerning this new covenant, he is simply proclaiming the essence of what God has always desired from His people—a personal relationship.

Ezekiel reminds every person that the Holy Spirit desires to begin a new work in them of God's grace and to establish an "everlasting covenant" with them (37:26). In his ministry, Ezekiel models this sensitivity and response to the Holy Spirit, and offers a look into the nature of God's dealings with the life of a devoted individual.

The Holy Spirit Fell on Ezekiel (11:5)

The phrase, "the Spirit of the Lord fell upon me" (11:5), is not unlike that used in the book of Acts to describe the encounter with the Holy Spirit by those in Cornelius' house (Acts 10:44). Both this Old Testament encounter and the New Testament reference identify a dramatic break-in of spiritual power in the lives of those present. In the case of those gathered at Cornelius' house, there is the spontaneous praise of God accompanied by speaking in tongues. Obviously, the impact of the "falling" of the Holy Spirit changed forever the course of the Gospel in opening ministry and salvation to the Gentiles.

In the case of Ezekiel, the descent of the Holy

Spirit on him is directly related to the prophetic message God had given him. The motive and compulsion to declare God's message was supernatural in nature, but very much within the scope of Ezekiel's anointing as a prophet to the nation.

This prophetic word was a direct challenge to the established structures of those who "give wicked counsel" (11:2). This impacting work of the Holy Spirit happened to Ezekiel, but it is something we can also expect *today*! The prophet Joel declared that when the Holy Spirit is poured out "your sons and your daughters shall prophesy" (Joel 2:28). Peter identifies this passage in Joel with the experience in Acts 2 at Pentecost (Acts 2:17). It is the outpouring of the Holy Spirit which releases prophetic gifts. And, it is the openness of the prophet to speak (Ezekiel 11:5) which allows God's intentions to be known by His people.

Ezekiel Sees Visions (1:1; 43:3)

Once again the presence of the Holy Spirit at work in the prophet is clearly attended with supernatural experiences. The prophet describes encounters which are so unusual that they can only be understood adequately as visions of spiritual things which he attempts to relate in terms of the language of his day.

This phenomenon of visions, as described by Ezekiel, has its counterpart in the New Testament. At Pentecost, Peter refers to Joel 2:28 to describe the widespread nature of God in giving visions to His people.

There is a false theological construction that limits God's desire to communicate with His people, or indicates that God has changed His mind about supernaturally impacting the lives of people. The Bible never hints that God no longer deals directly with individuals in supernatural ways. But it definitely offers words which direct our personal response to the gifts of the Holy Spirit.

The discerning of spirits (1 Corinthians 12:10) and the testing of the spirit of a prophet (1 John 4:1) are direct warnings of the potential for spiritual deception. The measuring stick of accepting words, visions, and supernatural encounters with the Holy Spirit is clearly outlined in God's Word.

In light of potential spiritual deception, what does the operation of a "gift" of the Holy Spirit reveal about our relationship to Jesus Christ (1 John 4:2)? What are the character and motives of those who declare a supernatural experience with the Holy Spirit (2 Timothy 3:1-7)? How does a prophetic word or vision align itself with the revealed truth found in the whole of the Bible (2 Timothy 3:13–17)?

These questions define the boundaries for a genuine work of the Holy Spirit, and as it was with Ezekiel, God still desires to communicate His heart to His people so that He may heal, save, and restore them.

A New Heart and New Spirit (18:31)

God promises judgment for "every one according to his ways" (18:30). But the answer for every individual is to "Repent...so that iniquity will not be your ruin." It is in this context that the prophet continues to declare: "Get yourselves a **new heart and a new spirit**" (18:31).

The prophecy that has gone out over Israel has the frightening implications of divine judgment. In the execution of judgment the Lord has shown Ezekiel the dreadful sword of destruction that will obliterate all who remain. The only answer and hope is repentance and the renewal made possible by the work of the Holy Spirit in each individual's life.

The Lord promises the establishing of an "**everlasting covenant**"(16:60; 37:26). "And I will set My sanctuary in their midst forevermore" (37:26)—the result of this covenant will be the blessing of God's everlasting presence. With the heart-rending declaration of God's abandoning the Temple, He now opens up a brand new understanding of how His presence can once again become accessible to His people. He is offering a way of escape in the midst of declared judgment. But this will take a personal renewal with God Himself at an individual level.

The promise to remove the "**stony heart**" and to bring the presence of a "**new spirit**" (11:19) will enable those who receive the everlasting covenant to walk in the statutes of the Lord and to forsake the ways of idolatry and sin. The ability to fulfill the demands of God's righteousness is not based on the ability to make or keep His covenant—God will make this covenant and, by the power of His Holy Spirit, He will keep those who open to it.

As revealing as any scripture in the Bible that shows the heart of God toward the lost is the one found in Ezekiel 18:32: "**For I have no pleasure in the death of one who dies … Therefore turn and live!**" The call to repentance and the promise of a new heart and spirit are deliverance from the spiritual death that destroys all who walk opposed to God. *It is a call to life!*

Ezekiel promises an "**everlasting covenant**"— and it is Jesus Christ who is the Mediator of this covenant to all those who will open to Him in faith (Hebrews 12:24).

RESTORATION OF THE LAND ACCORDING TO
EZEKIEL'S VISION

Nelson's Complete Book of Maps and Charts © 1993, Thomas Nelson, Inc.

PART 3

PRACTICAL WISDOM FROM EZEKIEL

JACK HAMILTON

GIVING HOPE IN THE FACE OF
JUDGMENT

Almighty God keeps His word. This is one of the most stabilizing facts in the universe.

When God speaks on a subject, the issue is settled. As for any promise made by Him, you can "take it to the bank." In a world where things are so changeable and short-lived, the Word of God is constant and steady (cf. 1 Peter 1:25). The reliability of God's word is a blessing to all humanity.

While this is a comforting truth, it is also a confronting fact. God not only gives promises to people, He declares commands that are to be obeyed too. If the conditions in the commands are fulfilled, then the fullness of the promise is realized.

God's desire for people is that they experience the benefits of His promises. When the conditions of the promises are ignored and deviant attitudes and acts replace God's expectations, then the consequences of disobedience are experienced. This is called the judgment of God. In reality, it is people being held accountable for their sins, and this execution of justice is faced by the offender.

What is true for the individual also has implications for a nation. When the cumulative sins of a people become so great and when the nation is called to repent and does not, then that nation faces the judgment of God. This is not suddenly decided upon by the Lord, but usually results from a people who stubbornly continue in a steady pattern of disobedience to the laws of the Lord.

This does not, however, nullify God's promises of blessing, but delays their fulfillment. God will continue to work with people in order to bring His word to pass. The generation that turns from the pattern of sin and disobedience will receive the benefit of God's promise to them. Nowhere in the Bible is this more clearly portrayed than in the book of Ezekiel.

Through the words of this prophet, we see the pronouncements of the judgment of God on Israel and the statements of promised hope to be realized in national restoration. While this may seem to be an impossible task, justice and mercy find compatibility in God alone.

The practical applications of Ezekiel for contemporary believers are these:
- The transcendence of God
- The reliability of God's Word
- The essentiality of God's glory
- Individual responsibility
- Expectancy in God

Embracing these realities will either protect us from falling or, like Israel, prosecute us before the eternal court.

VISIONS AND VISUALS

God is a communicator. He gives individuals messages to be passed on to others. These words from heaven are to inform, instruct, correct, and inspire (cf. 2 Timothy 3:16). In order to amplify what is being conveyed, the Lord gives His spokesmen images to be acted out.

Jesus spoke in parables, using common and everyday practices to underscore the truth He was talking about. As a result, listeners were astonished for He taught them as one having authority (Matthew 7:29). The use of this communicative tool gave understanding to the masses, for they could visualize what He was saying, and because they could understand, credence was given to what He said.

Ezekiel's messages came from Jehovah God. Not only did he declare what he heard, he also illustrated these communiqués by acting many of them out.

He was taken captive in the second deportation of Jews from their homeland to Babylon. He settled in a small community of exiles southeast of Babylon. Because he was a priest, he was known and looked up to. People came by his house, and many times they would find him acting out the word that had come from the Lord. These living illustrations made clear to all what God's message was to them:

- Judgment upon a rebellious and impudent nation was imminent.
- Justice would be exacted from the oppressing neighboring Gentile nations.
- And while all this was happening, a seed of hope relative to the return of those who were exiled, the restoration of the nation, and the rule of the Messiah was planted in the righteous remnant.

Much of the message was hard to hear but Ezekiel faithfully delivered these words over a twenty-five year period. What made him so persistent? It begins with the first vision—a view of God's attributes manifested by the vision of the holy cherubim.

In preparation for understanding this magnificent event, it is important to note three things from Ezekiel's testimony.

1. "The heavens were opened" to him (1:1).

This means that he was going to peer into the invisible realm. When God wants to communicate directly to people, He rolls back the curtain of heaven. At the baptism of Jesus, the Father acknowledges, "This is my beloved Son." But prior to the thunderous declaration "the heavens were opened" (Matthew 3:16-17). What Ezekiel was about to see and hear emitted from heaven. God was in direct communication with him.

2. "The word of the Lord came expressly" to him (1:3a).

What he was to repeat to others were not words of his imagination. Born by the Spirit of God, these words were of divine origin, for no true prophetic word comes by the will of man nor is it for private interpretation (2 Peter 1:20–21).

3. "The hand of the Lord was upon him" (1:3b).

This idiomatic phrase reveals God's acceptance and approval of Ezekiel. He is the right person, in the right place, at the right time. The central idea is that God is supervising and strengthening Ezekiel for this task. As a matter of fact, the name Ezekiel means *"God strengthens."*

It is overwhelming when the presence of God is felt by the human soul. Nothing is visible, but the reality of such an encounter is powerful. Now add to that the visuals of a dark cloud, illumined around the edges as if having backlighting from the sun. Lightning like fire is blazing all around. Out of the midst of this stormy scene a theophany is taking place. Four supernatural living creatures emerge representing the attributes of Almighty God.

It is this encounter that commits the prophet to the assignment. God is on the move, and He is going to utilize the dedication of Ezekiel to proclaim His message from what is thought of as a forsaken place.

The transcendent God is met. He is readily conveying His greatness and special nature to a man who will relay His message to others.

THE TRANSCENDENT GOD

God is out of the realm of normal human experience or expression. The word *transcendent* implies exceeding usual limits or extending or lying beyond the limits of normal experience.

When God chose to invade human space in visual form, it had be in some recognizable way. The vision recorded by Ezekiel in 1:4–28 uses words like "appearance" (vv. 5, 13–14) and "likeness" (vv. 5, 10, 13), because God was giving him a frame of reference to understand what he was seeing. So something like an electrical storm represented the glory of God. Creatures that had a combination of features known to the prophet represented the attributes of God.

It was Ezekiel's comprehension of these symbols that motivated him for his difficult mission. He had no doubt that it was God Almighty giving him this assignment, and he would be faithful in the execution of it because of this. This manifestation of the glory of the Lord formed the backdrop for all the announcements that Ezekiel would make.

Today's believer needs to take to heart the greatness of God. He is no trivial deity. Some contemporary attitudes are simply too casual concerning the Lord. He is not a kindly, old bearded grandfather in the sky. Encountering Him has the magnitude of the most amazing extraterrestrial episode one can imagine. Is it any wonder then, that the Bible declares, "Fear God and keep His commandments, for this is man's all" (Ecclesiastes 12:13).

A. *God is holy* (1:4, 13–14).
   Represented by fire, torches, lightning.
B. *God is everywhere present* (1:16–21).
   Represented by the wheels.
C. *God knows everything knowable* (1:18).
   Represented by the eyes in the wheels.
D. *God is all powerful* (1:24)
   Represented in the name "*Almighty.*"
E. *God is the incarnate Redeemer* (1:5, 10).
   Represented in the likeness of man and the four faces.
   1. Face of the man—Savior.
   2. Face of the lion—Baptizer with the Holy Spirit.
   3. Face of the ox—Healer.

4. Face of the eagle—Coming King.

THE RELIABILITY OF GOD'S WORD

Many of the best and brightest of Israel's people were captives in a strange land. They were taking solace in the fact that Jerusalem had withstood the assault of the Babylonians. However, they were ignoring the fact that the nation as a whole, and their leaders in particular, had violated repeatedly the covenant made with God back at Sinai.

When God formed the nation of Israel, the Mosaic covenant became their national constitution. It gave them instructions on how to live for God and experience His blessings. It also stated the consequences for disobedience to this covenant (Exodus 20–Numbers 9).

Unfortunately, the history of Israel was replete with its being influenced by its pagan neighbors, violating the Law of God, and becoming increasingly corrupted.

After dealing with the nation and its leaders for over five centuries, the line had been crossed. And it becomes Ezekiel's lot to say to them that God's stated judgment for their sinful ways is about to take place. Jehovah did not forget to bless during the periods of repentance and revival and has patiently withheld His wrath. It will not be so any longer, and the prophet is commissioned to declare this fact.

Two major judgment events are prophesied: the destruction of Jerusalem with its temple, and those taking refuge at either site will be destroyed too.

Ezekiel preaches incessantly to a people who found it difficult to believe that God would allow

Jerusalem to fall. While the Word of the Lord was doubted by many, God vindicated His Word through Ezekiel (Chapters 1–24).

The prophet of God then turns his attention to the nations who think they will prosper because of Israel's fall. Ezekiel also preaches lengthy, pointed oracles concerning their doom (Chapters 25–32). All that he said came about, accurate beyond the possibility of human invention.

The book of Ezekiel is a remarkable record of God's Word being true to the most minute point. This testimony to the veracity of the Word of God should stimulate believers living in today's world to be confident about all of the pronouncements of the Lord.

A. *The Character of the Judged.*
   Rebellious, impudent, stubborn, hard-hearted, wicked (2:1–3:27).
B. *The Content of the Judgment.*
   Siege, famine, pestilence, warfare/death, doom (4:1–7:27).

THE ESSENTIALITY OF GOD'S GLORY

The glory of God is more than brilliant light. The manifestation of His glory is a testimony to His presence. If any people ought to have understood this, it was Israel.

All during the trek in the wilderness, God's glory was visible to them. In the tabernacle there was the annual visitation of God's glory at the Mercy Seat. And finally, the remarkable manifestation of the glory of God was at the dedication of the temple built by Solomon. However, they disregarded this powerful expression of the presence of the Lord. They lived despicable lives in sight of God's glory.

Their doom is sure when God gives Ezekiel a vision of Jerusalem and the temple. He sees the spiteful and wicked expressions of idolatry on the temple mount. And then to his horror, the glory of God not only exits from the temple but from the city too!

There is a marked relationship between the presence (glory) of the Lord and His blessing. It was Moses who noted that if the presence of the Lord did not go with them, they would not leave the place where they were, no matter what was promised (Exodus 33:14–18).

The glory of God is not cosmetic. It is essential. His presence in the life of the believer gives confidence to bear the challenges of life.

Ezekiel bears the shame of the departure of the glory of God in the vision of Chapter 10. Later, he receives a similar vision and experiences the elation of the return of God's glory to a restored temple (Chapter 43).

INDIVIDUAL RESPONSIBILITY

There is a tendency today to avoid responsibility for our problems. The spirit of the victim is a convenient shift of blame for many. One the most significant contributions of the book of Ezekiel is the clear teaching that individuals are fully responsible before God for their own actions and not punished for the sins of others.

The Israelis had coined a cultural proverb to

escape their individual sense of responsibility for the calamities they were experiencing. *"The fathers have eaten sour grapes, and the children's teeth are set on edge"* (18:2). Its subtle message was that the present generation was not accountable for the disasters that had come upon them, but had merely inherited the conditions and problems that previous generations had set in motion. This thinking had a fatalistic element ("You can't do anything about the way things are") and perpetuated irresponsibility ("You don't have to do anything since it isn't your fault").

God says, "You shall no longer use this proverb in Israel" (18:3). He then states that, because of His involvement with people, everyone can be assured that His judgment will be fair and true. Only those who actually deserve to die because of their sin will die.

If one generation fails to stay faithful to God and is disobedient to His Word, it may leave a dangerous precedent of disobedience for the next generation. This unfortunate spiritual legacy, however, will not excuse the next generation. They may follow the pattern of their predecessors, but their disobedience is their own and not out of necessity.

There is a dual approach to dealing with sin. Confess sin, acknowledge you are guilty, repent, and turn from the attitudes and actions that are sinful. If people will do these two things they will be forgiven and live.

    A. *The Example of a Righteous Father and Son* (18:5–9, 14–17).

    B. *The Exposure of an Unrighteous Son and Father* (18:10–13, 18).

C. *The Explanation of the Righteous Standard* (18:19–28).

D. *The Entreaty to Repentance* (18:29–32).

EXPECTANCY IN GOD

When you're an exile for an extended period of time and you have had to be the purveyor of bad news, your world can be very discouraging. This is amplified when the things that offered a glimmer of hope are destroyed also. This is what Ezekiel experienced.

The one encouraging thing going for him was that he was being the messenger of God. He had been faithful in the execution of his responsibility. That did not, however, fully soothe his soul, until one day when the message and vision were different. It wasn't about judgment and destruction of the present, but of revival and restoration for the future.

It was full of hope in spite of the depressing realities of captivity—hope revealed in the plan of God to usher His people into a time of blessing and intimate relationship to Himself.

This must have had a settling affect on Ezekiel. He was privileged to see the new temple, a restored priesthood, caring princes, and most important of all, the return of the glory of God. The great hardship he had been carrying seemed lighter now because something superior to what he had known would be taking place in the future.

It has been said that a person can exist fifty or sixty days without food, seven to nine days without water, and four or five minutes without air. But without hope you cannot live for a second. At a time when society and culture seem to be in a severe decline, people need to have hope. When your personal world seems to be crumbling, you need to maintain hope.

The last nine chapters of Ezekiel are a message of hope. These words are a vibrant testimony that God has a wonderful future in store for those who will remain faithful to Him.

    A. *A Restored Temple for Worship* (40:1–42:20).
    B. *The Return of God's Glory* (43:1–12).
    C. *The Renewed Social Structures* (44:1–46:24).
    D. *The Recovery of the Land of Promise* (47:1–48:35).

JUDGMENT AND GRACE

Ezekiel presents some pretty amazing contrasts. The spirit of judgment is clearly seen. While this is a frightening reality, it is righteously applied.

At the same time, the glory of God's grace is expressed through the prophet. God takes no delight in the death of the wicked but calls all people to repentance unto life.

> ***"For I have no pleasure in the death***
> ***of one who dies," says the Lord God.***
> ***"Therefore turn and live!"***
> **Ezekiel 18:32**

LET'S LOOK AT EZEKIEL

WRITER: The writer of this book was Ezekiel the prophet.

PROPHET TO: The Jewish captives (exiles) in Babylon. (Many of Ezekiel's prophesies were about other nations as well as the Jews.) Ezekiel's message to the Jewish captives was that their captivity was the result of their sin. Before they could hope to return to their land, they must return to their Lord.

OTHER PROPHETS OF THIS TIME: Jeremiah, who remained with the Jews in Jerusalem; Daniel, who lived in the court of the rulers in Babylon. Daniel was taken captive to Babylon nine years earlier than Ezekiel. Ezekiel and Daniel were probably about the same age. Jeremiah was older. He had been a prophet for about 30 years in Jerusalem when Ezekiel was taken to Babylon.

TITLE: "Ezekiel" means "God strengthens." Ezekiel was strengthened by God for the ministry God gave him.

59

These pages are a simple pictorial summary of Ezekiel. They are placed here to introduce you to the resource mentioned on page 66.

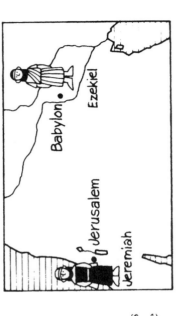

600 BC			593 BC		586 BC	580 BC
PROPHETS:	JEREMIAH (J)	DANIEL (B)		EZEKIEL (B)		
KINGS:			ZEDEKIAH (J)			

● = KINGS
(J) = JUDAH
(B) = BABYLON

JEWS EXILED TO BABYLON

FALL OF JERUSALEM

Ezekiel was one of the captives taken to Babylon. He spoke God's word to the captives there.

MAIN EVENT

■ EZEKIEL, A Prophet in Babylon

Chapters 1–48

Not all the people of Judah were taken to Babylon at the same time. For a while Jeremiah stayed in Jerusalem warning the people who remained there about the city's coming destruction. Ezekiel was one of the captives taken to Babylon.

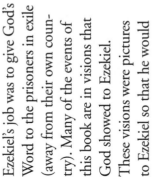

Chapters 4–24: By using special stories and actions, the prophet taught the people why God would destroy their city, Jerusalem.

Chapter 1–3: God called Ezekiel and gave him a job to do. Ezekiel heard God's words and told them to the people.

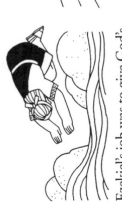

Ezekiel's job was to give God's Word to the prisoners in exile (away from their own country). Many of the events of this book are in visions that God showed to Ezekiel. These visions were pictures to Ezekiel so that he would know what to tell the people.

Some of the prisoners hoped they would be able to go home to Jerusalem soon. But Ezekiel told them this would not happen.

Chapters 25–32: Ezekiel said that other nations who did not listen to God would also be destroyed.

Ezekiel told the people that they will be led by a wonderful Shepherd. (This Shepherd is Jesus.)

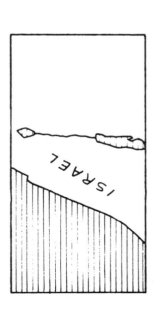

Chapters 33–48: Ezekiel gave the people God's good news. Someday the people of Israel will be gathered from wherever they are and made a great nation again.

63

USING AND GROWING WITH THE
BIBLE BOOK-A-MONTH STUDIES

The formulation of the ***Bible Book-A-Month*** concept was born in the heart of Dr. Jack Hayford to help people achieve three things: *systematic, substantial,* and *thorough* coverage of the Bible.

The Triangular Approach

There are many worthwhile approaches to a study of the Holy Bible—for example, "synthetic" study—which draws together highlights to provide a quick grasp of a book; "critical" study—which assesses the ancient textual resources that authenticate the trustworthiness of the book as a document; or "verse-by-verse" study—which seeks to exhaust every book of the totality of its content.

Distinct from any of these, the ***Bible Book-A-Month*** study seeks to achieve the maximum possible grasp of a book's truth, while keeping a pace forward which sustains the average Bible student's interest. It is <u>demanding</u> enough in its *academics* to seriously engage those interested in intelligent, thought-provoking study. Yet it is <u>dynamic</u> enough in its *movement* to avoid losing passion and to keep each student at a point of continuous anticipation.

This is done through use of a **"triangular**

approach" to each book—which focuses the three primary things to be found in every book of the Bible.

1. Each Bible book contains an *essential message*: the core concepts which distinguish that book and provide its place in God's Word.
2. Each Bible book presents *problems* and evokes *questions.* Good Bible study helps questioners find *satisfactory answers* to reasoned inquiry, even as it demonstrates the *relevancy* of God's Word and discovers the power of the Holy Spirit revealed in each book.
3. Each Bible book provides *practical wisdom* and *personal guidance*. In each book, *insights for faithful, fruitful pathways* will show how to adopt, adapt, and apply the Bible to your life, as Jesus' disciple.

Triple Tools—Support Resources

1. Each study is accented by a *pocket-sized book* as the one you have in hand.
2. Pastor Hayford is in the process of reading the whole Bible in the New King James Version on audio cassette. These can be ordered in conjunction with the *Bible Book-A-Month* program.
3. Overview teachings of each book are available on audio cassette as recorded live at The Church On The Way.

Additional resources, noted in each volume, can be ordered by calling Living Way Ministries at 818-779-8480 or 800-776-8180.

"This is a book you'll use over and over again as you study God's Word."
—**Billy and Ruth Graham**

WHAT THE BIBLE IS ALL ABOUT

Quick Reference Edition

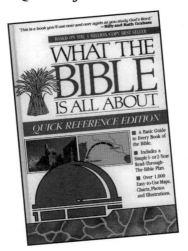

Here is a simple, direct way to study the Bible!

WHAT THE BIBLE IS ALL ABOUT covers everything from the beginning of time to the end of the world, and it gives you the basics of every book of the Bible quickly and concisely. It includes information on the writer of each book, timelines, charts, maps, concise summaries, key verses, and key people.   *softcover* **WBAA $9.99**

Unveil the Keys to Scripture!

HAYFORD'S BIBLE HANDBOOK

Hayford's Bible Handbook is an unparalleled resource that uniquely unveils the keys to Scripture, providing not only a wealth of information, but also a spiritual stimulus that will encourage your faith and service to Christ.

It unlocks Scripture with:

- Illuminating surveys of each book of the Bible.
- Helpful illustrations, time lines, maps, and charts.
- A complete Visual Survey of the Bible.
- An Encyclopedia Dictionary with over 1,300 entries that address subjects of particular interest to Spirit-filled believers.

This guide opens the riches of Scripture with a unique focus on practical ministry in the Holy Spirit's power—all to deepen your life in Christ.

reg. $24.99 **HBH $22.99**

Discover the roots of your faith!

THE JEWISH ROOTS OF CHRISTIANITY

To recapture the roots of our faith is to significantly enrich the quality of our spiritual lives. This video symposium creates an awareness of our Hebrew heritage and the benefits of a Hebraic perspective of our faith.

This video study series contains four VHS tapes with full study notes outlining presentations by Dr. Jack Hayford, Dr. Marvin Wilson, Dr. Frank Eiklor, and Rabbi Yechiel Eckstein. (4 tapes) **JRCVS $49.95**

ORDER FORM

Qty.	Item	Code	Price	Total
____	_____	___	____	____
____	_____	___	____	____
____	_____	___	____	____
____	_____	___	____	____
____	_____	___	____	____
____	_____	___	____	____
____	_____	___	____	____
____	_____	___	____	____
____	_____	___	____	____
____	_____	___	____	____

Postage and Handling

$0.00 - $9.99 . . . . $2.95
$10.00 - $29.99 . . . . $4.95
$30.00 - $49.99 . . . . $6.95
$50.00 . . . . 15% of Subtotal
Outside North America $8,
          plus 20% of Subtotal

Subtotal _____

Add 8.25% sales tax to CA orders _____

Shipping and Handling _____

Donation (Optional) _____

Total _____

Name _____

Street Address _____

City _____ State _____ Zip _____

Phone Number (_____) _____

Method of Payment: ❏ Check or Money Order ❏ Visa ❏ MC

_____/ _____-_____-_____-_____ / _____
      Signature   Card Number   Exp. Date

RESOURCES

LIVING·WAY MINISTRIES

14820 Sherman Way, Van Nuys, CA 91405-2233

Please call for prices and ordering information:
1-800-776-8180 • 1-818-779-8480

Please include your remittance (U.S. currency only) with order.
Make check or money order payable to Living Way Ministries.

SOUNDWORD
Tape Subscription Service

Join hundreds of others in subscribing to the SoundWord™ TAPE OF THE MONTH program. A key message by Pastor Jack is selected each month and sent to your home for systematic instruction and encouragement.

Annual Albums from our TAPE OF THE MONTH program are also available. Each contains 12 powerful teachings by Pastor Hayford. Ask about the subscription or album series when you write or call.

1-800-776-8180

LIVING · WAY
MINISTRIES

And be sure to ask for a copy
of our 120 page Ministry Resource Catalog!
It is available for purchase, or as a bonus
when you place an order.